Contents

Contributors

Kent Ford is the technical producer of whitewater instruction videos *Solo Playboating!* and *The Kayaker's Edge*, available from most whitewater shops and catalogs.

Laurie Gullion is the author of *Canoeing* and the American Canoe Association's *Canoeing and Kayaking Instruction Manual*. Director of the Undergraduate Program in Sport Management at the University of Massachusetts, she has paddled six thousand miles along Arctic rivers.

John Shepard is a writer and an American Canoe Association instructor-trainer who lives in St. Paul, Minnesota.

Bruce Morser, a Colgate University graduate who also holds a Master of Fine Arts from the University of Washington, has won many awards for his unique illustrating style. He lives on Vashon Island, Washington.

Canoeing

Edited by Dave Harrison

Illustrated by Bruce Morser

STACKPOLE
BOOKS

0 11557 02722 8

Copyright © 1998 by Stackpole Books

Published by
STACKPOLE BOOKS
5067 Ritter Road
Mechanicsburg, PA 17055

Printed in the United States

First edition

10 9 8 7 6 5 4 3 2 1

Cover design by Tracy Patterson

Illustrations © 1990–1997 Bruce Morser. All rights reserved.

The material in this book originally appeared in *Canoe & Kayak* magazine. See page 60 for subscription information.

Library of Congress Cataloging-in-Publication Data

Canoeing / edited by David F. Harrison—1st ed.
     p.   cm.—(Canoe and kayak techniques)
  Collection of articles originally published in Canoe & Kayak.
   ISBN 0-8117-2722-X (pbk.)
   1. Canoes and canoeing. 2. Kayaking I. Harrison, David, 1938– . II. Canoe & kayak. III. Series.
GV783.c195 1998
797.1'22—dc21
                                                97-26190
                                                    CIP

Introduction

Many Americans believe they were born with a paddle in their hands. True, the canoe is part of our cultural heritage, but, to the best of our knowledge, good canoe technique is *not* genetically or culturally transmitted; it's learned. Nor is it intuitive, especially when you are faced with a wind-tossed lake or a set of rumbling rapids.

A day spent floating down a placid stream or poking about on the marshy fringes of a quiet lake can be highly satisfying, but in order to get beyond the arboretum (so to speak), you must master certain skills. The canoe is a simple craft, and that is perhaps its highest virtue. And capable—especially when you find out canoes have crossed continents, navigated all the coasts of North and South America, and run the Grand Canyon—both ways! The skills needed to paddle such diverse conditions are not simple, and even though you may not aspire to such epic journeys, there are unlimited adventures awaiting those who do put the time and effort into mastering canoe skills.

You will see in the following pages images of both solo and tandem paddlers. A common configuration is the man in the stern ("I'm the captain!"), his spouse or pal in the bow. Believe us, tandem paddling is a tough way to learn how to canoe. If possible, it's best to learn to paddle a solo canoe, and to learn *all* of the strokes and braces, on both sides of the canoe. The ideal is to have a tandem team who have each mastered the strokes in a solo canoe; then, the pair is not only complementary, but interchangeable between bow and stern. More importantly, they understand that each paddler is responsible for his or her end of the canoe.

Going Straight

Kent Ford

You probably know the feeling of trying to go straight with a boat that seems to have a mind of its own. The boat veers and spins into an even tighter turn.

Good quality strokes at the stern will always correct this veering. Think of the front of the boat as being pushed into the turn, so you have to correct from the stern. With the bow lined up on a distant landmark, going straight requires persistence and, more important, anticipation. Armed with two strokes, the stern pry and the stern draw, you can turn in either direction—to get going straight again.

The most powerful correction stroke is a well executed stern pry. A good stern pry starts with the paddle blade plastered against the boat, toward the stern, with the blade angle vertical for maximum bite. To get your blade in this position, the thumb on your t-grip hand will be on top. Get the t-grip out over the water. The pry itself is a short, six-inch jab out to the side, using the gunwale as a fulcrum. This stroke is powerful and effective.

Often it is best to pause until you feel pressure on the blade before initiating the pry motion. To make a major correction, do several short prys.

It is my opinion that nearly half of all intermediate and advanced paddlers have poor stern prys. These are prys that stray too far from the boat, or the blade is more flat than vertical; both have a negative effect on forward speed. You may develop this bad habit because it feels less stable to have the blade in the correct position, which is far back and close to the boat. Sometimes the result is that bow draws are overused; a paddler figures out, or is taught, that strokes at the stern are slowing him down. In truth, what slows him down are poorly executed stern strokes. Only when you have mastered efficient steering from the stern should you attempt correcting from the bow.

To correct in the other direction, use a stern draw. The paddle blade should travel in an arc to the stern, starting about two feet from the boat. Keep both hands below shoulder level, and be sure that the entire blade remains submerged throughout your stroke.

Watch your blade sweep throughout its arc to the stern. This will involve your torso power. Pay close attention to the blade angle. Without your making the adjustment, the blade has a tendency to twist at the end of the stroke, reducing its bite on the water. Transfer the power into your boat by pulling your hip toward the blade.

Learning to correct from the stern using these simple techniques will help you have more control and fun on the river.

The Solo C

John Shepard

Just as a river will go out of its way to carve a circuitous route to the sea, left to its own devices a solo canoe hasn't much regard for straight-line travel. And if you're like the rest of humanity, your first solo strokes are likely to send you spinning in circles.

To understand why, consider that your position at midships places your strokes far from the canoe's keel line. If, on the other hand, your canoe had a slot eight inches wide along the keel through which you could reach the water for a forward stroke, your canoe would show much greater interest in tracking the straight and narrow. But it has no such slot, so chances are that even your best J-stroke will have the effect of a sweep executed from the stern of a tandem canoe: the craft will turn away from your paddle. Don't fret, though, for Rx is but a C-stroke away.

The C-stroke, like the J, gets its name from the pattern that the blade follows in the water when the stroke is performed on your starboard side; the same move on the port side traces an inverse C.

From a catch position that's a comfortable stretch ahead and a foot or more out from the gunwale, trace the top of the C by drawing the blade beneath the bilge of the canoe and converting to a forward stroke. This pulls the bow of the canoe to your on-side, counteracting the forward stroke's tendency to spin the canoe in the opposite direction. Reaching under the bilge places the forward portion of the stroke as close to the keel line as possible. Note that in order to reach the blade beneath the bilge, your grip hand must stretch far out over the gunwale until it is "outside" your shaft hand.

As the blade passes beneath your right knee, begin converting the forward stroke into a powerful J-stroke. Complete the C pattern by moving the blade from beneath the bilge and away from the side of the canoe, making sure that the power face of the blade (that side of the blade that meets the greatest resistance from the water during a forward stroke) meets resistance from the water throughout. Like a traditional J-stroke, point the thumb of your grip hand down and away from the canoe. Applying leverage during the J pushes the stern back into your desired line of travel. Complete the stroke with a feathered above-water recovery.

The C-stroke is especially useful if you're starting from a dead stop, when the canoe is especially susceptible to turning. You can reduce the corrective features of the C once you are under way and apply more of your precious energy moving the canoe where you want it to go: forward.

Reaching under the bilge places the forward portion of the stroke as close to the keel line as possible.

To Go Faster, Paddle in Molasses

Kent Ford

To go anywhere in this sport, you need to be able to develop speed from a standstill. But the fact is, forward paddling is a major weakness of ninety percent of the boaters on the river.

The common fallacy is that the paddler pulls the blade through the water on a forward stroke. Think of it this way, instead: Plant the blade firmly in the water and pull your hips to the blade, a subtle but important difference. Think of your boat as gliding in a giant vat of molasses. Each stroke should stick in the molasses, so you have a firm blade to pull against. When you simply pull the blade through the water, you don't get firm resistance on the blade, the blade slips, and you can't pull yourself as far.

The blade and molasses analogy provides the answers to many commonly asked questions about the length and speed of forward strokes. The farther forward you plant the blade, the greater the distance you can pull yourself forward. Don't pull until the blade is fully immersed. Once the blade reaches your hip you can't pull yourself forward any further; that's the logical point to finish the power phase of your stroke.

Simply increasing your stroke rate won't necessarily make your boat go faster. To go faster, concentrate on pulling harder while keeping the blade stuck. Then, recover quickly to the next plant.

When you first learned to paddle forward, you probably used your small, nimble arm muscles to provide all your power. A better strategy is to incorporate larger muscles for a more powerful, efficient stroke.

Imagine sitting in your boat and reaching forward to start a lawn mower. This twisting reach—or rotation—will unleash the torso and hip power you need on the water. But don't mistake a forward lean for rotation. Too much front-to-back motion causes the boat to bob and inhibits control and efficiency. Torso rotation, by contrast, involves twisting your shoulders to provide the pull for each stroke. To wind up for the stroke, lead with the chest on your paddle side. Then concentrate on getting the blade crisply in the water before you pull your hips forward. Strive for a smooth, gliding sensation.

Remember, as well, to keep the paddle shaft vertical throughout the pull phase. The farther the blade wanders from the side of the boat, the more your stroke resembles a turning stroke.

To apply power, make sure your paddle has a good hold on the water; don't just yank on the paddle. Bubbles or splashes behind the blade are an indication you are pulling too fast.

To put these concepts into practice, do some flatwater paddling alongside a series of fixed points such as dock pilings or buoys. Watch the blade and monitor how much it slips with each stroke. Strive for firm resistance against the blade.

One way to check your stroke efficiency is by following and mimicking a really smooth paddler. You can also practice the forward stroke mechanics in front of a mirror and monitor your actual torso rotation (as opposed to what you think you are doing). Develop the paddling rhythm on dry land before you have to worry about your stability and keeping your boat straight.

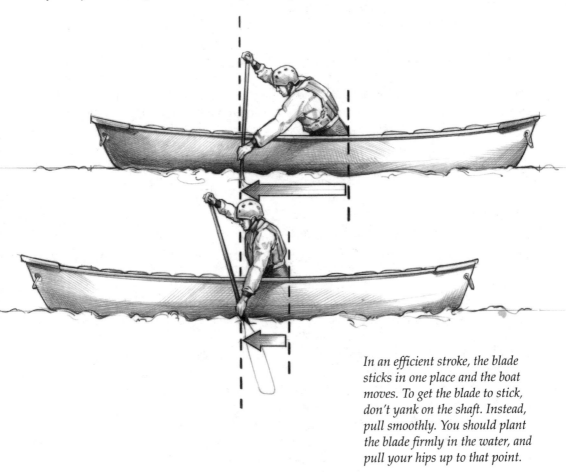

In an efficient stroke, the blade sticks in one place and the boat moves. To get the blade to stick, don't yank on the shaft. Instead, pull smoothly. You should plant the blade firmly in the water, and pull your hips up to that point.

The Cross-Forward Stroke

Laurie Gullion

Stalling out is the curse of solo canoeists who want to make a jump from paddling flatwater to handling fast currents. Do you ever feel like the river world is moving faster than your boat? You may know where you want to put the boat but lack the necessary boat momentum.

Boat stall-out is most commonly experienced in exiting (and entering) an eddy. If you stall out on the eddy line, wobble through the boils, or fail to pierce the eddy line near its top, then your biggest problem is a lack of speed. The slower you go, the more time you give the eddy line to grab and hold onto your canoe.

The key is aggressive straight-line paddling without resorting to momentum-killing corrective strokes. The goal is to paddle forward as hard as possible from a dead stop and maintain momentum for ten strokes. The cross-forward stroke is used to generate momentum and control boat direction. Here is a series of steps on flatwater to get you on the fast track.

First, set a straight-line course by focusing on a shore object—that will be your destination. Then position your canoe anywhere from 45 to 90 degrees—the greater the rocker of your canoe, the larger the angle—offset from the straight-line course. You are anticipating, and avoiding, the natural spin of your canoe away from your normal (or on-side) pad-dling side. Now, execute several hard boat spins back onto a straight course toward your destination and switch to forward strokes on your on-side to maintain speed.

Let the bow spin about 5 to 10 degrees past the target object, so the canoe is slightly turned toward your on-side. You can maintain this position as long as you have the boat leaned slightly toward the paddling side. As soon as the bow starts to swing toward the target, execute a J-stroke to prevent the canoe from spinning off course. Don't wait until the boat is pointed toward the target. That's too late. Anticipate the natural spin and make an early decision to prevent it.

A change in boat lean is crucial as you switch from the cross-forward to the forward stroke. During the cross-forward, the boat leans toward the stroke. Reaching aggressively forward and leaning sharply at the waist will force you to shift weight onto the knee nearest the paddle. A good boat lean also slows the boat's spinning effect and prevents it from moving back onto the course line too quickly.

A weight shift also occurs when you switch back to a forward stroke on your on-side, with more weight resting on the knee closer to the forward stroke. Again, the lean will keep the boat turning slightly toward the paddle and arrest the boat's spinning effect.

Why use the cross-forward for momentum? The answer is in the total-body action required to execute the cross-forward stroke. The torso compression and raising of the upper body to pull the paddle through the water engage the large trunk muscles, and you should feel an explosive burst of power. It's stronger than a forward or J-stroke to get started. The cross-forward is not a subtle stroke, however. Once under way, it's best to use forward strokes and J-strokes with boat lean for subtler adjustments in direction.

The cross-forward stroke is not a subtle stroke.

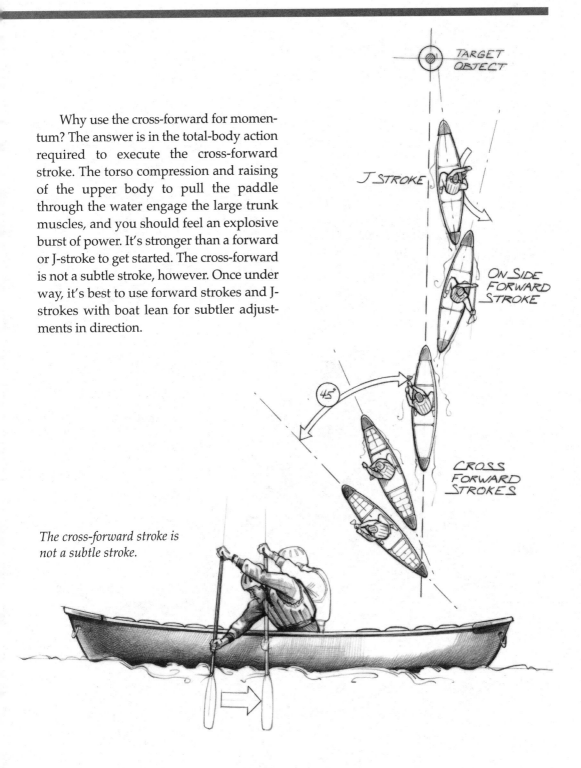

TARGET OBJECT

J STROKE

ON SIDE FORWARD STROKE

45°

CROSS FORWARD STROKES

How to Travel Sideways

Kent Ford

Moving sideways is a necessary part of canoeing. Maybe you're at a lake, trying to pull alongside a dock. Or perhaps on a river, trying to slip out of the path of an obstacle or cozy up to shore. Regardless, moving sideways with ease can be as frustrating as parallel-parking your car without bumping into something.

Canoes are meant to go straight, not sideways, so your strokes have to be very definitive to make the boat respond. The simplest way to move sideways is with the draw stroke. Turn your torso so you place the blade straight out from your hip. With both hands over the water, try for a good bite on the water, with the blade

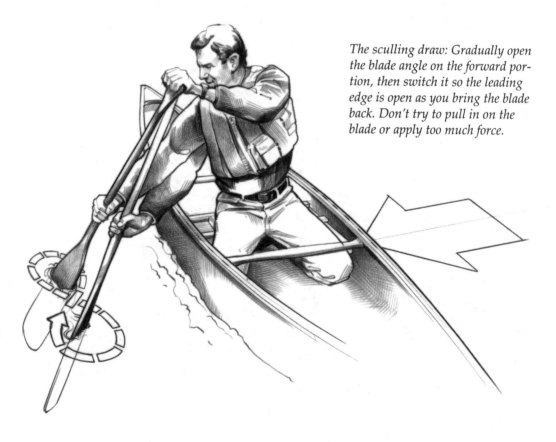

The sculling draw: Gradually open the blade angle on the forward portion, then switch it so the leading edge is open as you bring the blade back. Don't try to pull in on the blade or apply too much force.

digging in deep. Then, pull the blade in gently, holding your top hand steady as you do. Feather the blade 90 degrees to slice it out for the recovery. Tilting your boat slightly away from the stroke allows it to slide sideways more easily, and more importantly, it provides counterbalance so you can hold both of your hands over the water. This helps position the blade to pull the boat to the side, not push down on the surface.

The sculling draw is a variation of the draw stroke. It accomplishes the same lateral movement of the boat but with better paddle control and finesse. As you move the blade through the water, subtle changes in blade angle provide maximum sideways pull on the boat with minimal resistance to moving the blade.

First work on basic sculling. Gently move the blade along a 3- to 4-foot line 6 inches away from your boat, making sure to keep the shaft straight up and down. Gradually open the blade angle on the forward portion, then switch it so the leading edge is open as you bring the blade back. Don't try to pull in on the blade or apply too much force.

Do you have basic sculling mastered? Try these variations either alone or with your partner: sculling to pull the bow around, then the stern. Try cross-bow sculling with the same variations—sideways, to the bow, and to the stern. If you master that, try sculling the other direction by reversing the blade angles.

With a little practice you will be able to "parallel park" effortlessly, and you will notice the rewards of better finesse.

Side Slippin'

John Shepard

For all its pointy-endedness and sleek lines, the canoe is clearly a vessel designed to move gracefully fore and aft. But sometimes a sideways move is just what's needed, like when you want to cozy up to shore, or when you're barreling along and a boulder looms in your path.

If your canoe is sitting stationary in the water and you want to move sideways—let's say to reach a nearby dock—you have a couple of choices. The first is for the paddler whose blade is on the same side as the dock to do a series of draw strokes.

The alternative is for the dock-side paddler to execute a sculling stroke.

In the scull, the blade is planted where it would be to start a draw, then sliced back and forth, forward and aft, along a line roughly parallel to the keel line. As it's moved in this way, the power face—that side of the paddle blade which meets the greatest resistance from the water in a forward stroke—continually

meets resistance from the water at about a 45-degree angle. The scull requires no recovery and results in a continual sideways movement of the canoe.

To complement either of these moves, the partner paddling on the other side can execute a series of pry strokes. Say you're cruising along and spy a rock oncoming just below the surface. You can use a stationary version of the draw and pry to cause the canoe to "shift" position, or move diagonally forward without changing the alignment of the keel line. For the stationary draw, plant your paddle as you would for a normal draw but rotate the blade 45 degrees, so the approaching water will deflect off the power face of the blade toward the canoe. Similarly, begin the stationary pry by placing the blade at the start position for a regular pry, or in a rudder position slightly aft. Then angle the blade about 45 degrees so the non-power face deflects the oncoming water away from the canoe.

If the bow does a stationary draw while the stern, paddling on the opposite side, does a stationary pry, the canoe will shift toward the same side the bow is paddling on. Reverse the strokes, and the canoe will shift the opposite way.

In Praise of Going Backward

John Shepard

Getting somewhere in a canoe, as in life, usually means forging ahead. Going backward has all the wrong connotations: retreat, humiliation, failure.

But don't be fooled. The more competent you are paddling your canoe backward—that maligned direction where the eyes are useless and instinct betrays you—the better you are traveling forward, sideways, or any direction you might choose.

Paddling backward is a little tricky, and to master it requires a fine sense of paddle sensitivity. You have to anticipate the movement of the canoe just *before* it happens, then precisely apply just enough leverage to turn things your way. Paddling with truly heightened sensitivity is a high and noble way to go through this world.

So, get your partner to the pond and start paddling backward in a straight line. Notice that roles now are reversed: the bow paddler is in the best position to alter course while the stern paddler can best supply the power. We'll coach them one at a time.

The stern paddler, now in the leading end of the canoe, provides power with reverse power strokes. These employ the same elements essential to a good forward stroke, only in reverse. Wind up your upper body by rotating the torso, plant your blade not far from behind the hip, uncoil yourself, and stroke backward

maintaining a vertical paddle shaft, using the non-power face of the blade (the side of the blade that meets the least resistance in a forward power stroke). Then remove the blade from the water a comfortable reach ahead of you and feather the blade back to plant position.

Meanwhile, the bow paddler, now in the trailing end of the canoe, uses reverse J-strokes and reverse sweep strokes to keep on track. The basic dynamics for the reverse J are the same as for the reverse power stroke, except that after beginning the stroke you need to carve the paddle blade beneath the bilge of the canoe—crossing your grip hand well out over the gunwale—to gain leverage for the final, corrective part of the J (once under way, corrective action becomes more subtle). Turn the thumb of your grip hand down and away from you so that the non-power face of the blade continues to meet resistance from the water throughout the stroke. Recover with a smart feather.

The reverse sweep is a mirror of the forward sweep. The non-power face of the blade is at work. Accentuate the final part of the stroke where the blade is being drawn toward the stern of the canoe. This is where the stroke is most powerful.

Peering over your shoulder to see where you're going makes for poor paddling form and deprives you of the opportunity to practice guiding the canoe more by feel than by sight. Watch the wake and paddle swirls stretching out before you and base your corrective strokes on how well aligned you are to that watery line.

With a little practice, the bow paddler should be able to anticipate and maintain a perfectly straight course. And when that happens, you know you'll be getting somewhere after all.

Lean and Mean

John Shepard

In learning to make full use of your canoe's hull shape through judicious leans, the old saw holds absolutely true: Nothing ventured, nothing gained. What's ventured is a dry state of equilibrium that you may well be fond of. To be gained is much-improved performance, sharpened "survival skills," and some good paddling fun.

The basic idea is to emulate an infant learning to walk. She teeters, then falls. She holds tight, steps out and falls again. And with each tumble, she takes a giant step toward mastering body control, balance and applied geography.

Similarly, without discovering the precise limits of balance in your open canoe by exceeding them, you'll never have access to the full range of maneuvers of which you and your craft are capable. You'll also never become fully "at home" in your canoe, and you'll have poorer responses when you're thrown off center by a passing wave or an untoward passenger.

On a warm sunny day that is doubly blessed with warm water, don your swimsuit and shove off into thigh-deep, calm water solo or with your partner. Kneel comfortably, leaning against your canoe's

Lift your paddle from the water and complete the turn by leaning the canoe gunwale to the water.

seats or thwarts, knees wide apart. Relax. Keep breathing.

With paddles stowed and working in harmony with your partner, rock the canoe slowly side to side by pressing alternate knees downward, keeping your upper body upright. Do this until the canoe capsizes and repeat the exercise several times. You may discover a particular point at which your canoe loses its stability (some designs have more pronounced balance points than others), though this may not be until after water has begun pouring over the gunwale.

Next, slowly rock the canoe side to side again, stopping each time at the balance point or when the gunwale is just about to take in water—whichever point you reach first. Hold the canoe in that position for longer and longer intervals until you can do so comfortably for a slow count of 10. Again, the key is to relax and keep your upper body erect. As tenuous as

this position may seem at first, it is the point at which your canoe has the shortest keel line, and is thus most maneuverable. The more at ease you can be with your canoe on "edge," the snappier and more graceful will be your turns. You also will have far greater poise at this most critical point of a potential capsize.

Finally, let's add some motion. Propel the canoe straight ahead with a series of forward strokes, then initiate a turn to one side with a powerful turning stroke in the stern. Lift your paddles from the water and complete the turn as best you can by leaning the canoe, gunwale to the water. This maneuver is easier solo, as less weight at the ends facilitates the turning motion. Practice this move while leaning radically toward both the inside and the outside of the turn. Leaning to the outside may seem especially precarious at first— but then so did your pioneering steps when you were just a toddler.

"C" for Yourself: Lean Into Those Turns

Laurie Gullion

Muscle building isn't one of my primary goals in canoeing, but energy conservation is. Given a choice between a high- or a low-energy turn, I'll choose the efficient one every time. Leaning your canoe is a skill worth developing whether you are headed for flatwater or whitewater, and it will advance you beyond sluggish, energy-intensive turns.

You might first object to a canoe that isn't straight upright, but you can develop confidence by daring to lean your boat, especially if you start with some practice in shallow water.

Tilting your canoe on its side lifts the ends of the canoe out of the water, which reduces drag and increases the amount of canoe rocker. Imagine your boat looking

A leaned canoe turns faster; the ends are out of the water and rocker increases.

more like the bottom of a rocking chair, a shape which lets you turn, even spin, your canoe in the water.

It is important that you lean your boat rather than your body. Keep your body upright, head up, and tilt the boat under you. The trick is to transfer your weight without relying on your paddle for support. Alpine and cross-country skiers know the concept of weight transfer in making turns. Just as the skier shifts weight from one leg to the other leg by pushing off his ski, the canoeist pushes down each knee or buttock to effect a weight shift. There needs to be a corresponding lift of the opposite knee or buttock. The result is a body position—sideward, not hunching—that resembles a "C."

That "C" position lets you maintain an upright upper body. If you were to lean out over the water instead, the off-center motion could land you in the water. An off-center lean may work for a motorcyclist banking into a turn, but in the water, where the physics are vastly different, you need to keep your body centered over your canoe.

The transfer of pressure using your knees and butt to create the "C" pushes the canoe down in the water, which displaces and lets the canoe roll slightly on its side. The more you transfer this weight and press down, the more pronounced the "C" in your torso, and the greater the boat lean.

Try practicing your boat leans in shallow water. You can even plant your paddle blade on a shallow bottom; then, practice loosening up your hips and letting the boat rock from side to side under your body. Practice solo, or work with a tandem partner to coordinate your leans. When you feel comfortable, move to deeper water and combine boat lean with turning strokes to increase the speed of your turns. You can time your spins from both an upright and the leaned position and see for yourself how a leaned boat turns faster—if your muscles haven't already been convinced!

Levering the Gunwale

Laurie Gullion

I never thought small hands would be a liability in paddling, but consider the pryaway stroke. I find it a problem, as do many small-handed kids and women.

The pryaway is a powerful turning stroke that uses the gunwale for leverage rather than the body (which, in my case, is what I would politely call sturdy). But my small hands are the weak link in the system, so I'm always looking for a better way.

The pryaway forces me to get a better grip on the paddle to control its movement. During the stroke, the paddle is vertical to the water surface, the shaft resting against the gunwale, ready for action. You must maintain a point of

The paddle shaft is the lever; your hand and gunwale are the fulcrum.

attachment between the shaft and the gunwale in order to keep pulling in on the paddle grip, which pries the blade away from the canoe and moves the boat away from the paddle. The shaft hand creates the fulcrum.

Big-handed people have no problem with the task. They simply slide their shaft hand around the paddle shaft and the gunwale and press the two points together. They often have inches of fingers to spare, and they can even tuck their thumbs under the gunwale for insurance. Their hands function as a kind of oarlock to keep the paddle vertical against the gunwale.

Small-handed people must improvise. I grip the shaft fully with my hand, resting the heel of my hand on top of the gunwale. The arm stays bent at the elbow, at a right angle, and tucked against my side; then my body helps keep the shaft against the canoe. It's a total hand/arm system at work.

Because I keep my arm against my torso, the stroke happens nearer my body, just in front of my hip. (Big-handed people often execute the stroke nearer their knees and can take better advantage of the rockered end of the canoe.)

Two other strategies give me additional insurance: I'm ruthless about the catch position for the stroke so that I can take maximum advantage of the lever, and my pryaway is an extremely short one so that I can control the paddle more easily.

At the catch, I place the paddle blade as far under the canoe as possible, and my top hand on the paddle grip is well out over the water. This position allows me to grab water directly under the canoe.

I pull the top hand toward the center of the canoe to pry the water, but I stop the stroke when my top hand comes just past the gunwale. This moves the blade only a small distance from the canoe without its leaving the water, and the paddle stays vertical to the water surface. Most importantly, the paddle shaft doesn't move away from the gunwale, and my arm stays locked in the right-angle position. Avoid a long stroke; otherwise the blade may lift near the water surface, reducing your leverage and dragging the hand away from the canoe.

Crossing Over

John Shepard

"And last of all, don't forget to keep your paddles on opposite sides of the canoe at all times." What beginning canoe course *doesn't* include this well-worn advice? But in each of us there's a rebel who secretly delights in defying such authority. The cross-bow draw, or cross-draw for short, satisfies this demon.

Let's say you're in the bow, paddling on your left side, approaching an eddy to your right into which you intend to turn smartly. These are the perfect circumstances to defy your instructor's dictum and deliver a dazzling cross-draw. There are several tricks to executing this wonderfully contorted stroke properly. To get

the hang of it you may want to grab a paddle, kneel comfortably on the floor, and go through the motions as you read this.

First, you have to torque your body around dramatically since your lower (or "shaft") hand has to extend across your body and out over the opposite gunwale—quite a reach. At the same time, your grip (or "control") hand should wind up directly in front of you at about forehead height. To ensure that your body is appropriately torqued, turn your torso so that the zipper of your lifejacket is facing the shaft of your paddle throughout the maneuver.

The angle of your blade when it's planted in the water just after you cross the eddy line also is critical. The paddle's power face—the side of the blade that pulls against the water during a normal forward stroke—must be rotated to face the tip of the bow, at about a 45-degree angle to the keel line of the canoe. To gain the proper angle, twist the wrist of your control hand so the thumb of that hand is pointing directly away from your face. You may notice once your blade is properly planted that the eddy current exerts considerable force against your paddle. Hold tight, keeping the paddle shaft as vertical as possible, until the resistance lessens and you can draw your blade toward the bow. Once you've drawn your paddle to the side of the canoe, pull the boat up into the eddy with a cross-forward stroke, then switch back to the other side. Throughout the turn you needn't concern yourself with controlling the lean of the canoe, as your partner in the stern—who, alas, is missing the fun—is in a much better position to do this.

The Open Canoe Roll

Kent Ford

Rolling has become a common skill for open boaters paddling continuous class III and harder rivers. Rolling saves the long swim, and keeps you in the relative safety of your boat.

When you first try to roll, you will probably focus on the paddle motion. This isn't the essence. Instead, the key is rolling the boat up with your lower body, while your paddle supports the torso. Then your paddle helps you move up over the boat. Good rolling depends on this hip and torso rotation. Torso and knee motion is what rights the boat.

The best way to learn this is with your hands on the side of a pool, or resting in a friend's hands at water level. Put your head on your hands. To roll on the right, practice moving the boat through the full range of motion. To wind up, stretch your torso to the surface, at right angles to the boat. Follow through by gently pressing your forehead toward the water and tugging up on your right knee. Try to minimize the force by being light, keeping your weight floating near the surface. Doing this effortlessly is a prerequisite to rolling with a paddle.

The low brace roll uses this same torso and knee motion. To learn the low brace roll, try this easy system. First, float the paddle perpendicular to the boat on your paddle side. Then tip over toward your paddle and curl your body up so you can grab the shaft. Really stretch your torso for the surface. Try to turn so both shoulders are near the surface and over the shaft of the paddle. Your head, hand, and paddle blade should clear the surface before you start the rolling action.

Now drive your forehead down toward the shaft, and push with your hand while you pull up on your right knee. Push down on your left knee. Starting with your shaft arm bent and gradually straightening it will give you a little extra power, but your body should do most of the work. This will feel gradual at first; if the paddle starts to slip when you press on it for support, turn your torso and hips. Each step happens incrementally.

To finish, pull the t-grip across in front of your waist, while sweeping the blade forward. When the gunwale clears the surface, swing your head low and across the gunwale to the other side. Think of scratching your nose on each gunwale of the boat. People often spoil a roll by raising their head too soon.

Once you're rolling consistently on a low brace, it's time to learn the setup. This way you can roll no matter which way you flip. The setup is with your body tucked forward and the blade flat against the top of the boat, ready to swing with your body out to the side.

A good way to learn this is in a decked C-1, where the force required is typically less. Converting a decked C-1 roll to an open boat requires a little more force and a little slower roll.

Your boat design and outfitting can affect the ease of rolling. Outfitting should be snug but allow easy escape when necessary. If you can slide your knees or bottom more than one inch in any direction, your outfitting is probably too loose. Some boat designs and float bag configurations can make the boat get stuck just short of upside down. When this happens, you'll need a short underwater sweep stroke to pull the boat completely upside down.

A closely related skill is the brace. When properly used, this skill can often save you from flipping in the first place. With some practice, you can develop a brace, a roll, and save the hassle of a long swim.

The body and paddle are aligned perpendicular to the boat; the torso and knee motion rights the boat.

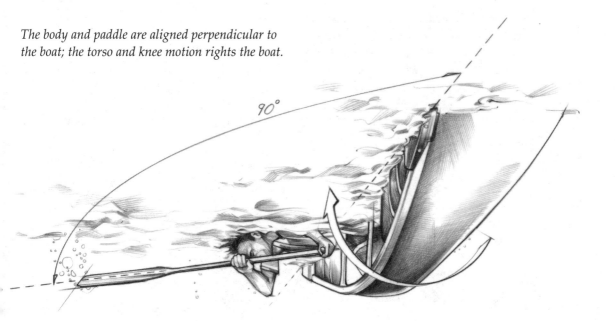

Brace Yourself

John Shepard

Watch a pair of skilled paddlers work their way through a chaos of river waves and you'll see that they roll with every punch, their paddles ready to catch themselves if they're thrown off balance. They know that no matter what the river dishes up, they have two nearly bomb-proof defense responses: the high and low brace.

These two "static" strokes serve flat-water paddlers just as well. In fact, these strokes are essential to the repertoire of anyone serious about paddling the occasional tippy canoe. We'll look at them one at a time.

The low brace works like a stabilizing outrigger, saving you from capsizing toward the side you're paddling on. The non-power face of the blade (the side of the blade that meets the least resistance from the water in a forward paddling stroke) is extended perpendicular to the canoe and flat against the surface of the water. In this position, the paddle can support a surprising amount of weight before the blade sinks into the water. The trick is to make the best possible use of this momentary support to quickly right the canoe.

Kneel on land with paddle in hand and mark some imaginary gunwales on either side of you. Extend your paddle perpendicular to your imaginary canoe's keel line with the non-power side of the blade facing the ground. Your grip hand should

High brace

Low brace

26

be out past the gunwale on the opposite side, knuckles facing groundward. Then tip yourself off balance toward your paddle and allow your grip hand to touch ground first, followed by the rest of the paddle. Right yourself by smartly pressing the blade against the ground. Practice this on land, then on shallow, calm water until you're comfortable extending the paddle far out to the side of the canoe, allowing the paddle to support your weight. Let yourself discover your limits by exceeding them.

If you can do a stationary draw stroke, there's really nothing more you need to master the high brace. The paddle position is the same, except that the blade is parallel to the keel line of the canoe and you can allow your grip hand to be positioned comfortably in front of your chest rather than out over the gunwales. This relaxed posture is a good running position in rapids, as you can easily apply an aggressive brace or quickly switch to another stroke.

The high brace comes into play when the canoe tips away from the side on which you're paddling. If that happens, you can "grab" the water with a draw stroke that keeps your weight in balance. With your partner complementing this move with a rock-steady low brace, you'll be a strong match for whatever mischief the river has in store.

Tandem Low Bracing

Laurie Gullion

One of my favorite coaches divides athletic endeavors into two categories. Some activities require speed, strength, and aggression (football and slalom skiing), while others use balance, coordination, and spatial awareness (gymnastics and diving).

Let's put tandem canoeing on flatwater in the second category. The activity is often a balance of technical skill and attitude; nothing requires more cooperation and coordination than bracing a tippy canoe.

Tandem paddlers can test their bracing skills with a simple exercise that requires balance, coordination, and spatial awareness. Think of it as a water ballet with all the ingredients of a classy freestyle maneuver.

First, each paddler should practice the basic reverse sweeping low brace to review the key ingredients: horizontal paddle shaft position, knuckles downward so the power face of the blade faces the sky, body weight resting primarily on the knee closer to the paddle (not the paddle), a smooth and slow movement of the paddle.

Now, both paddlers should prepare to execute the reverse sweeping low brace on the same side of the canoe. The exercise is a test of both bracing technique and the paddlers' ability to cooperatively control boat

Tandem bracing drills require commitment and coordination.

lean. Absolute coordination is needed, or the boat will flip (part of the fun)!

With the boat in a neutral, upright position, where is each paddler's body weight? Equally distributed between the knees and centered in the butt. As soon as they begin to brace, their weight shifts to the knee and buttock closer to the paddle. This weight shift also tilts the canoe.

When does the weight transfer occur during a reverse sweeping low brace? A slight shift occurs at the beginning of the brace and gradually increases to the point of maximum weight shift—when the paddle is perpendicular to the canoe's centerline. Here, the brace is the strongest because the paddle is at a 90-degree angle to the boat. You should feel pressure on the blade, but not body weight. The weight is felt on the knee closer to the paddle.

At this point, each paddler needs to simultaneously and smoothly push down on the "high side" knee and lift the "low side" knee to right the canoe. This action is a signal to end the brace and slide right into a forward stroke as the canoe returns to a neutral position.

Use this sequence to keep the exercise flowing: a reverse sweeping low brace into a forward stroke converted to a J-stroke (which leads right back into another brace). Focus on timing, synchronization, and smoothness until you can eliminate any bobble in your boat lean or any surface skipping in the brace. If the paddle skips across the water, you are rushing the move.

Lean the Boat, Not Your Body!

Kent Ford

INSTRUCTOR: "Lean, lean, LEAN!"
STUDENT: "I am leaning."
STUDENT'S THOUGHT: *"If I lean any more, I know I will flip."*

This scenario is often played out in whitewater canoeing and kayaking classes around the country. Leans, and the resulting good balance, are an important part of learning to paddle, but are rarely described with precision. Leans can be organized into three basic shapes: the J lean, the bellbuoy lean, and the body lean.

The "J" lean, named for the "J" shape of your spine, is a boat lean with your body weight centered over the boat. This lean keeps most of the weight off your blade so you can use it for balance and for strokes. The "bellbuoy" lean is named for the stiff rocking action of an ocean bellbuoy. Navigation bellbuoys are so bottom-heavy that they are self-righting. Boats aren't that way! So bellbuoy leans in a canoe or kayak require support from the paddle. As we will see, this makes it a less usable whitewater lean. The final lean, the "body" lean, leaves the boat flat while the body leans. Beginners like this lean since the boat stays securely flat. Of course that usually defeats the purpose. This frequent misunderstanding underscores the importance of describing exactly the type of lean required for each whitewater maneuver.

Sometimes beginner paddlers are fooled into thinking they are leaning the boat when in fact they are just leaning the body. This is actually just opposite to the correct J lean, since the boat is flat and the body is leaning out over the water. Instructors refer to this as the "I'm leaning, I'm leaning," for the replies students shout when told to lean more.

Learning and practicing the J lean are best done on flatwater. First lean your boat, and feel how the weight and pressure change from both knees to one knee. Thrust out your ribs and physically torque up the opposite knee. Notice how a good J lean requires that your head be cocked away from the direction of lean. If you can hold that lean for a while, try paddling forward while you maintain a slight J lean. Transferring this drill to mild rapids will be even better for developing your whitewater balance.

Canoeists often have a bad habit of riding their braces down rapids. These paddlers use their brace as a crutch, and thus immobilize the paddle for proactive strokes. The irony is that the brace most of these people use is really similar to a bellbuoy lean. True, without the blade in the water they would flip, but that is because they have a bellbuoy lean, not because they have a successful brace. You should be paddling with a minimum of braces, so your weight is balanced over the boat and so your strokes can be effective.

Eddy turns and peelouts are another showcase for proper leaning technique.

The J lean, the usual whitewater lean

The bellbuoy lean up against a rock

The wrong lean

Practice them without using strokes to adjust the turns. You will learn to feel the hull of the boat smearing across the water, sticking to initiate a good turn. It may feel more dynamic to do a turn with some of your weight riding on a brace stroke, but in the long run this impairs the effectiveness of corrections you can do with the blade. The faster the currents, the more you'll need to tilt your boat to remain balanced. As you finish the turn, gradually shift your weight onto both knees to flatten the boat.

Paddlers often develop a misconception about what sorts of leans are required in the middle of a jet of current. To understand correct leaning, think of standing on a moving sidewalk in an airport. Do you need to lean when you are moving along? No . . . only just when you step on or off the conveyor belt do you need to compensate differently with momentary leans. The same is true for whitewater. You only need to lean when you are in transition from an eddy to the current, or from the current to an eddy.

In small eddies, practice floating sideways with no lean so that you are comfortable as you and your boat bob up and down. Your weight should be low in the boat: shared between your knees and butt. You can add new twists to this drill by spinning in circles as you drift through standing waves. Only if you encounter holes (that stop the boat's momentum) or rocks (remember that bellbuoy lean!) will you need some sort of a lean.

Good balance on whitewater is really nothing more than understanding how to keep your body weight centered over the boat with proper leans. When we step onto a moving sidewalk, these leans are quite automatic, so we describe them as balance. Work on some of the mentioned balance and leaning exercises, and you will be amazed at the improvement in your paddling. The masters in this sport don't rely on the paddle for support, even with the boat on edge.

The Downstream Ferry

John Shepard

As a canoeist, you have three ways to relate to a river's downstream rush to the sea: paddling gonzo-style, faster than the current; surrendering to the current's pace; or slowing down until the river is actually passing you by. Though each has its time and place on a downstream run, the last option isn't as frequently used as it could be, because it requires skills with the contrary moves of the downstream ferry.

The downstream or "back" ferry allows you generous time to position yourself on your chosen route as you move sideways across the river while facing downstream. It shares the same basic principles common to the upstream ferry, but it calls for reverse strokes and eyes in the back of the head.

Rather than starting in an eddy, as is common for an upstream ferry, downstream ferries are most easily practiced while in mid-stream. Slow your pace with some backstrokes, and angle the canoe so that the upstream, or stern, end is pointed toward the side of the river that is your intended destination. The appropriate angle will vary with current speed and the strength of your paddle strokes, but about 15 degrees relative to the current is a rough guide. Maintain your angle, lean slightly to the downstream side of the canoe, power backward with reverse strokes, and you'll find yourself slipping neatly across the river.

The trick to this maneuver is that it's difficult to gauge and control the canoe's angle relative to the current, because the current is coming at you from behind—where you can't see it—and your moves all are reversed. Also, because the upstream end of the canoe meets the greatest resistance from the current, the bow paddler is in the best place to control the boat angle but in the worst position to see the canoe's alignment.

For the bow paddler to pull this off calls for supreme confidence in the reverse J and sweep strokes, occasional use of the draw and pry, and openness to taking direction. The stern paddler, whose main function is to crank out a series of reverse power strokes, can best see how things are going and thus can guide the bow's actions.

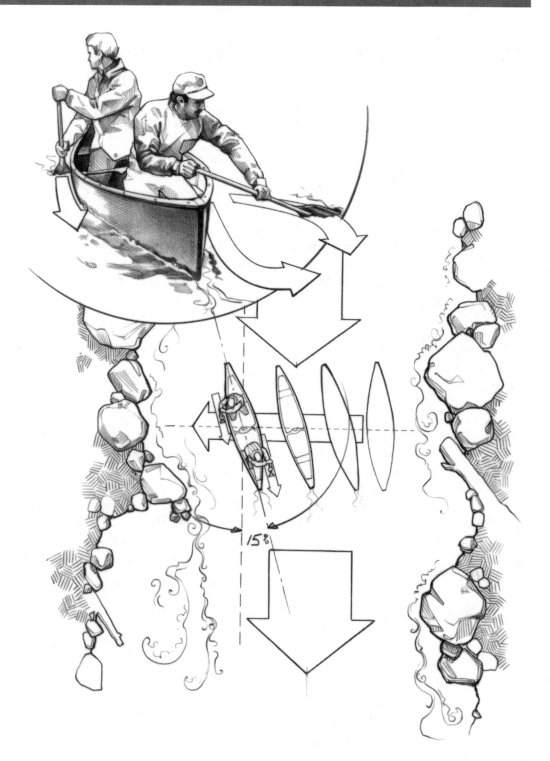

15%

The Solo On-Side Eddy Turn

John Shepard

The solo paddler gets to wear many hats. From solo position at midships he or she must serve as both bow and stern—not to mention lookout, engine stoker, and bailer. Take, for example, the on-side turn.

The solo on-side turn calls for one of two complex strokes that involve functions normally undertaken by both tandem partners. Executed properly, it will get you into and out of eddies with grace and style.

On a calm stretch of flat water (the best place to first practice your whitewater moves), work up a forward head of steam. Initiate the on-side turn with a strong C-stroke. Swing your feathered paddle forward in an above-water recovery, rotate your torso so that your chest is facing the paddle shaft, then plant your blade in the Duffek position: a comfortable reach ahead and about one and a half feet away from the side of the canoe. Your paddle's blade should be angled at about 45 degrees relative to the keel line of the canoe and rotated so that the power face deflects the oncoming water toward you.

As the canoe begins to pivot around your paddle, lean into the turn and draw your paddle forward and toward the side of the canoe. The blade should reach the canoe in the catch position for a forward stroke, which you can now execute to complete the maneuver.

You will have done a good job if you pivoted the canoe about 90 degrees from your former course. In mild current, as shown in the illustration, if you approached a decent-sized eddy with an appropriate amount of speed (a couple of power strokes is all you need) and crossed the eddy line at the right place (near the top of the eddy) and angle (about 45 degrees), the same move would spin you about nicely in an abrupt about-face.

If you're charging with some speed into a small eddy, however, make a slight addition to this stroke sequence. In this case, the reverse sweeping low brace replaces the above-water recovery between the C-stroke and the Duffek. As the paddle is pushed away from the side of the canoe in the final part of the C, continue the outward push while turning the blade over so that its non-power face is on the water surface (the non-power face is the side that meets the least resistance from the water in a forward power stroke). Extend your grip hand past the gunwale and, with knuckles of both hands touching the water and the shaft as close to horizontal as possible, sweep the blade in a wide arc until you reach the catch position for the Duffek. You'll need to give your paddle blade an inclining angle to keep your paddle on the surface during this sweep. You should also be sure to initiate the reverse sweeping low brace only after the bow has entered the eddy current to prevent spinning a neat circle in the main current while the eddy slips you by.

Your paddle's blade should be angled at about 45 degrees relative to the keel line of the canoe and rotated so that the power face deflects the oncoming water toward you.

Peeling Out

Laurie Gullion

One of my favorite river maneuvers is a peel-out because I enjoy the sensation of surging out of the eddy and riding away with the main current. The more turbulent the water, the more exciting the peel-out.

However, the turbulence lurking just beyond the eddy line can create some instability just when I want to feel "connected" solidly to the water and in control of the peel-out. The crucial moment occurs when I switch from the forward strokes that propel me out of the eddy to the Duffek, which braces and turns the canoe downriver. I'm reluctant sometimes to lift the paddle free of the water to plant it in the Duffek position, especially when the eddy line is boiling beneath me.

I have learned to test the water by switching to an underwater recovery after a forward stroke just as my canoe crosses over the eddy line. With my paddle in the water the entire time, I can clearly feel the change from the eddy current to the main downstream current, and it prepares me for the change in intensity.

It's the best offense-defense I can use. I'm paddling forward madly to crash through the eddy line, but my constant contact with the water creates a stable, secure posture. The underwater recovery is actually a backward slice through the water. As the forward stroke ends, I roll the thumb of my top (grip) hand back toward my body, so that the power face of the blade is now facing the canoe. I slide the paddle forward and past the eddy line out into the turbulence, until I can feel the force of the downstream current. Following a curving path slightly outward from the boat lets me smoothly prepare for the beginning of the Duffek (see illustration).

I gradually cock my wrists back toward my body to angle the blade and expose the power face to the oncoming current. I open up the power face against the downstream current only as much as its direction or strength demands. By maintaining this constant contact with the water, I can react subtly and quickly to what the current is doing against the blade, because I can feel every little change in water force. Finding that perfect brace position, where the blade is perpendicular to the oncoming water, is less of a guess with this "feel-as-you-go" approach.

I've found this different sensory clue to be enormously helpful with new paddlers who have problems seeing the current direction and estimating where to place the Duffek as they exit the eddy. The visual approach just doesn't work for them, because they can't see the current lines in the main flow. By the way, this same approach also works in entering the eddy.

Remember these tips to make the underwater recovery work. During the

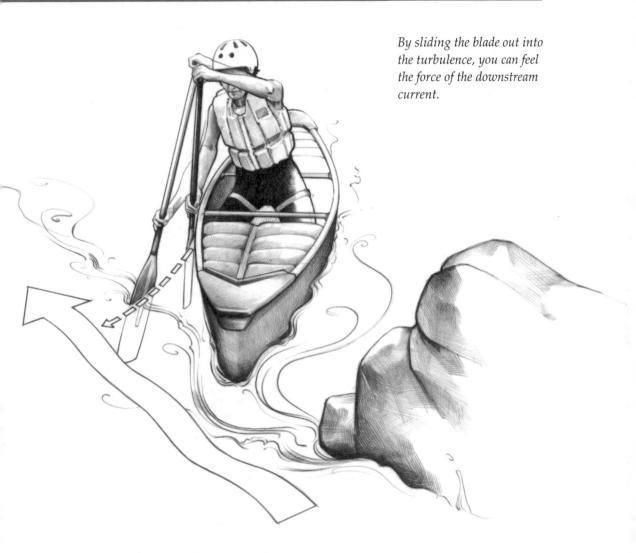

By sliding the blade out into the turbulence, you can feel the force of the downstream current.

recovery and the transition to the Duffek, keep the shaft vertical to the water surface so the blade is deep in the water, creating a solid brace.

Be forceful in slicing the blade through the water into the Duffek. Roiled water may try to have its way with the paddle, and you may need to make quick adjustments as the paddle gets pushed around. Push right back to pop the blade into the main current, where it will catch the downstream flow. Away you go!

Running Dry:
How to Handle the Huge Waves

Kent Ford

It is a beautiful, crisp spring day on your favorite run. So far you have stayed dry, as splashes from the choppy waves spray harmlessly aside. But around the corner is "House Rock" drop, your nemesis. Your gut tightens as you visualize the bigger waves that could swamp you, dampen your spirits, and make a swim much more likely.

There are several strategies for keeping your boat dry. Route choice should be your *first* choice. Look for the ramp of smooth water through the drop, sometimes referred to as a "window." These windows normally occur just off to the side of a wave train, or between the eddy line and the waves. Ride the shoulder of the waves until the waves are small enough for your boat to ride up and over. From your perspective in the canoe, looking downstream, the shoulder is that side of the wave that tapers off toward the shore or eddy line. Wave trains which build to a crescendo rather than diminish leave you with two alternatives: Take the final plunge, knowing that you'll take a lot of water into the boat (not a serious problem in a pool drop river), or eddy out just as the final wave crests.

If you find yourself in the midst of a wave, angle your boat 45 degrees to the wave and lean the boat, which will block the water from splashing in the downstream gunwale. Tilt the boat by lifting one knee, keeping your body balanced and centered over the boat.

Angle the canoe so that your paddle is on the upstream side of the boat, where you can catch your balance with a brace, if necessary. With the paddle in this position you can also execute a sweep to straighten out the boat. If you have angled your boat to block the waves with the paddle on the downstream side, use a bow draw to pull your boat over the wave and straight. Try to go with the flow. Drift through the rapids like a cork as you turn or bounce your boat to block the tallest waves.

River trippers carrying heavy loads often use a back ferry to keep waves from crashing into their boats, and for weekend whitewater warriors, momentary back ferries may give you a breather as you seek a dry line or safer route. Backstrokes sometimes work as a last-ditch effort to keep a wave from breaking over the bow. Putting on the brakes is a worthwhile skill, but it shouldn't be your prime mode for staying dry or running rapids.

These tricks will help you stay dry when you would really rather not be soaked. But with a warm day, good paddling companions, and proper equipment, there is nothing wrong with plowing through a few huge waves. In fact, it can be a lot of fun!

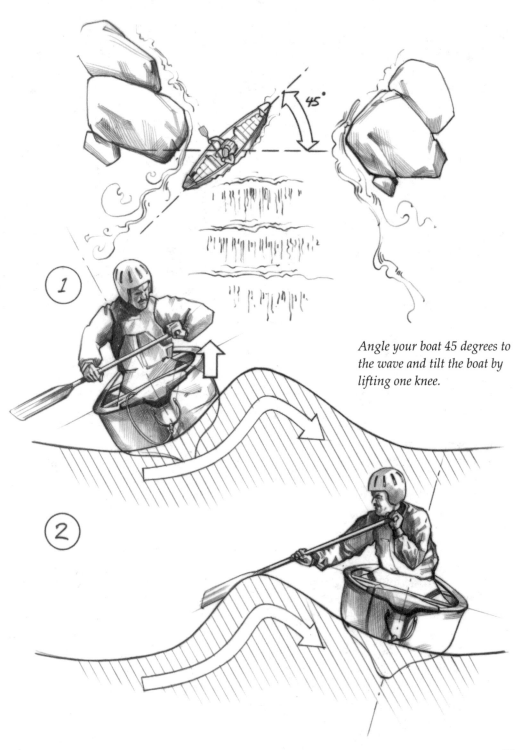

Angle your boat 45 degrees to the wave and tilt the boat by lifting one knee.

Wind and Waves: Strategies for Steering

Laurie Gullion

Wind makes even a small lake an exciting excursion for canoeists, but a familiarity with waves can make even a whimpering dog (or your partner) want to ride the big ones back to shore—and like it!

That's assuming the wind is blowing you back to your launch site. Another scenario is more likely, especially after a lazy lunch and a sun-drenched snooze on the shore. Your wake-up call is a mile-long paddle into the wind.

First, let's talk about paddling directly into a headwind. It's not a bad situation if the wave troughs are wide and sloping. Then your canoe will rise on the crest, and slide down the face of the wave nicely. This is the stuff of dreams. Just lean back to lift your bow so it doesn't cut into the next wave, and enjoy the ride.

The more realistic situation is gusty, intermittent blasts that create short, choppy waves. Your canoe falls off the wave crest and slaps the next wave, as water repeatedly slops over the gunwales.

In this situation the best strategy is to angle your bow away from a straight-ahead charge so that you take the waves at a slight angle. Keep your hips loose, let the canoe rock gently in the waves, and water over the gunwales will decrease. Slightly elevate the gunwale closest to the chop to stay even drier.

With the canoe now at an angle to the oncoming waves, you are perfectly positioned to ferry against the wind. As the wind pushes against the exposed side of the canoe, you need to paddle forward maintaining an optimum angle. The greater the exposure of canoe to oncoming wind (that is, the wider the angle), the faster you'll move sideways. Use landmarks to gauge your movement, and you'll know how hard to paddle and how much boat angle to set against the wind.

Ferrying against the wind is helpful for moving into the lee of an island, where you can rest up before heading toward shore again. In some cases, a wise strategy is to ferry away from your destination until you reach a protected shore; then, paddle next to the shoreline back to the launch site (see illustration).

You may sometimes use a tacking strategy similar to sailing. Paddling broadside to the wind, which often means the canoe is rocking sideways in the wave troughs, you will reach a point where you can quickly turn the canoe and run with the wind behind you. Riding the waves provides an exciting cowboy finish.

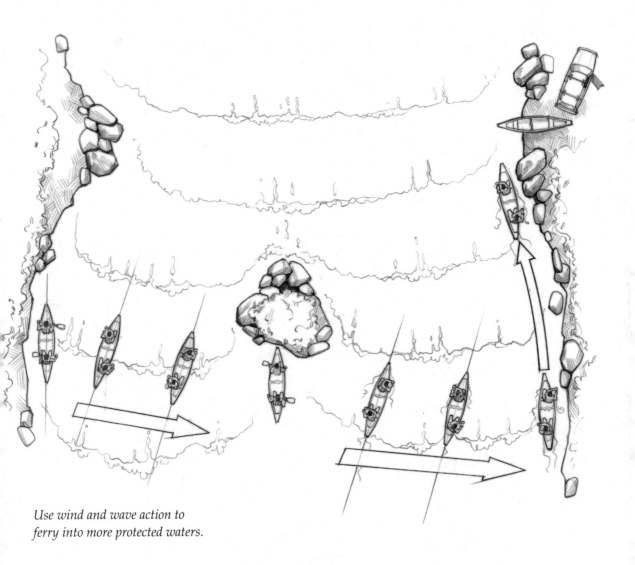

Use wind and wave action to ferry into more protected waters.

Running Loaded Boats

John Shepard

Smart ballplayers swing weighted bats before stepping up to the plate so their usual sticks feel light. Most wilderness canoeists, however, practice whitewater moves in a boat stuffed with little more than air. Then they paddle into the backcountry to run remote rapids in a loaded canoe that's as responsive as a moving van.

If you've ever followed this strategy, you know that negotiating wilderness rapids in a loaded boat is a different game than a full-flotation whitewater frolic by the side of the road. Mistakes are usually more costly; the sheer weight of a loaded canoe means much more work with less to show for it; momentum takes longer to

build—and to stop. And your margin of error diminishes with the amount of available freeboard.

Anticipation, thorough scouting, and well secured, waterproofed packs are keys to smart river running in loaded open canoes. Especially at the start of your trip, plan your routes carefully from shore and keep them simple. If the landscape is different from what you're used to, you may be fooled by differences in scale—the river may be wider, the current faster, and the waves bigger than they first appear. So give yourself plenty of advance time to set up your position at the start of a rapid. Also, since you can't

count on being able to jump into every passing eddy on a whim, plan your rest and scouting stops carefully.

If your skills are well developed, you'll find that moving slower than the current and using downstream ferries are good strategies for maintaining your position and staying under control. Plan your eddy turns far in advance and remember that boats with reduced freeboard call for judicious leans. Expect to discover that the unsettling side-to-side rocking sensation you sometimes experience as the canoe comes to a rest in the eddy will be more pronounced. Also, when you're ready to venture back into the current for an upstream ferry or peel-out, don't expect to be able to accelerate as quickly as you're used to.

Of course, all this doesn't mean that running rivers in a floating moving van can't be fun. Practice close to home with firewood-filled packs and you'll see that challenge and excitement are still there, you just need to work a little harder. And if you finally get tired of laboring under all the extra weight, you can always portage your gear and run the boats through high and dry—the way the river gods intended that they be run.

The Upstream Game

John Shepard

If eddy-hopping upstream sounds like all work and no fun—like the whitewater equivalent to climbing stairs—then maybe you're not yet fully acquainted with one of your prime moving-water allies: the often subtle power of eddy currents. In its rush toward the sea, water always seeks the path of least resistance. In climbing a rapid, you want to do the same thing. By taking advantage of offset eddies, whose tails and heads are aligned so that you can work your way upstream among them simply by ferrying back and forth, your route upstream may require no struggling at all against the downstream current.

If you're new at this, pick a class I–II rapid with distinct mid-stream and shore-line eddies. Though you'll begin your ascent from the bottom of the rapid, scout from the top first if you don't have a good view of the entire stretch from its base. Plan your route by selecting the sequence of eddies that will form the rungs of your upstream ladder, starting with the one at the top. Mentally working downstream from here, you can avoid the mistake of climbing to an eddy surrounded by downstream currents so powerful they'll blow you back to the bottom.

Once you figure out a string of eddies that will boost you from bottom to top

without having to buck a downstream chute that's too big to handle, you're ready to begin. The main skill required in this game is the upstream ferry. To review its critical features:

1. Keep the angle of entry into the downstream current low (10 to 15 degrees, with 0 degrees being straight upstream).

2. Exit the eddy with a head of steam and be ready with a powerful corrective stroke in the stern to counteract the pull of the downstream current (which will tend to turn your ferry into a peel-out) as your bow crosses the eddy line.

3. Lean slightly downstream and back, toward the stern of your canoe, to keep from being rolled upstream and to reduce the pull of the current's purchase on your bow stem.

Finally, use the shape and forces of the eddies to your best advantage. Once you're within the clutches of an eddy's tail, let up on your strokes and allow it to pull your boat upstream. Though your upstream movement may be initially slow, take a few relaxed strokes as you catch your breath. Then, when you're ready to climb the next rung of the ladder, accelerate and use the eddy current to propel you, like a cagey old salmon, out the very top of the eddy and into the downstream current once again.

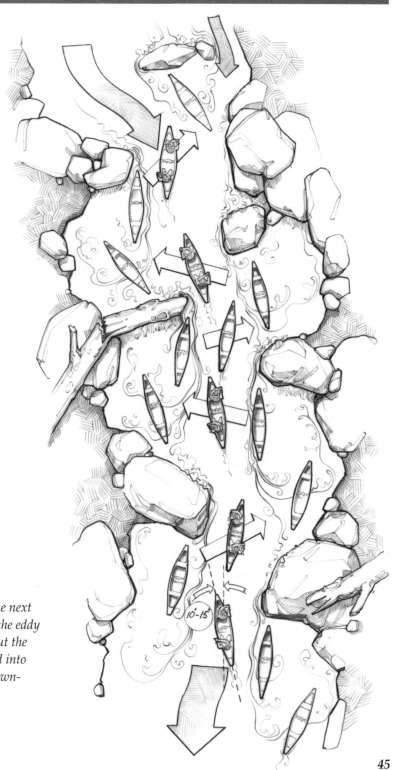

To climb upstream to the next rung of the ladder, use the eddy current to propel you out the very top of the eddy and into your ferry across the down-stream current.

10-15

Surf's Up! Perfect Your Stern Draws and Prys

Kent Ford

Learning to surf can be frustrating and get you wet. Even if you have a feel for the current speed and boat angle, you still need to get onto the wave; otherwise, as soon as you cross the eddy line the current will send you downstream if you're not ready with a solid correction stroke.

The most common correction strokes are the stern pry and stern draw, which allow you to control your angle as you ferry and carve back and forth on the wave. A good stern pry starts with the blade plastered against the side of the hull, positioned about two feet behind your hip. Use a vertical blade angle for maximum bite. The thumb on your t-grip is just out over the water. Then, pry with a quick, 6-inch jab out to the side, using the gunwale as a fulcrum.

A stern draw moves the front of the boat in the opposite direction of a pry. Place the blade behind you and about two feet out from the side of the boat, with the blade rotated for maximum purchase on the water. Then pull the stern of the boat to your blade. Push out with your top hand and watch the blade to make sure it comes within an inch or two of the hull.

But if you want to get really good at surfing, you'll want to apply subtle strokes that take advantage of all the water rushing past your boat. Active strokes and poorly executed corrections can add drag and pull you back off the wave. The next time you're watching boaters at a surfing wave, notice how the hot surfers use *stationary* stern and pry strokes to control their angle on the wave. They can control their movements with blade angle alone. The blade, always in the water but moving only slightly, acts like both a rudder and a skeg on the wave; the paddle itself is almost static during the stroke.

The best method for perfecting stationary strokes is to have someone hold your bow painter so you don't move downstream. (It's ideal if your spotter can stand on a footbridge several feet above an easy current.) First, get in the stern pry starting position. Angle your blade very slightly away from the boat and twist the top of the t-grip away. Switch to the stationary stern draw by punching your top arm out and rotating the top of the t-grip toward your boat. The blade should be nearly under your boat.

To practice these strokes on flat water, get some forward speed, and then plant the blade in the stern pry position. Twist the blade very slightly until you feel the boat turn initiating, then punch out your t-grip hand and cock your wrists up to switch to the "stationary" stern draw. You can use the same general idea to do "shifts" and move your boat over several feet while it moves forward. Simply plant the blade—gently—opposite your hip.

Experiment to maximize the turning force on the blade while minimizing the drag. Translate the resistance on the blade to the boat through your knees and hips. As with many strokes, it is important to twist your torso toward your paddle side to keep power on the stroke. With practice, you'll be able to lock in on surf waves and control your critical angles.

A good stern pry starts with the blade plastered against the side of the hull, positioned just behind your hip. Use a vertical blade angle for maximum bite. Your t-grip hand should be just out over the water, thumb on top. Make a quick 6-inch jab out to the side, using the gunwale as a fulcrum.

Ferry Tales:
Doing Your Homework

Kent Ford

Ferries get you across the river, and better yet, get you to some great surf waves. In your first whitewater class you probably learned about angle, speed, and correction strokes as the key elements to a good ferry. The slight angle to the oncoming current, along with speed across the eddy line, set you up to move smoothly across the current.

Well, at least it moved the instructor's boat smoothly across to the other side.

Starting a ferry can feel like a failed school exam. In a flash, the current grabs the front of your boat and spins you downstream.

To pass this test, you have to do your homework!

Doing your homework means putting your boat in position before you take the first strokes of a ferry. To set your ferry angle, you need to position yourself nearly parallel to the eddy line.

This requires good paddle control and finesse. You might have to back up; then, use draws or sculling to move your boat into place.

Once you are positioned close to the eddy line, study the current direction and speed. The current next to the eddy line has usually been deflected by rocks, so it flows in a different direction than the main flow. You need an angle of attack that will move your boat across the current. That might be 15 degrees to the first current that will hit your bow. The goal is to keep your bow from getting blown downstream. The correct angle depends on the speed of the water; the faster the current, the more you'll need to point straight upstream. If you are unsure of the angle, pointing upstream is more conservative.

The critical moment occurs as you pierce the eddy line. Part of your boat is in the eddy, and part is in the current, exerting different forces on your boat. Good forward speed reduces the time these forces have to alter your course.

Stroke timing and placement are important. The instant your bow reaches the oncoming current you should be poised for a stern draw, or stern pry correction, in case you feel your boat turning downstream. To maintain your balance, you will want a slight boat tilt as well.

If your ferry is intended to get you on a surf wave, you need to know exactly where to aim when you leave. Aim for the depression on the eddy line, in between the peaks of the waves. This is where the trough of the wave meets the eddy. If you hit upstream of this low spot, your bow will plow into, or ride up the oncoming wave. Then, the oncoming ramp of current will force your bow to turn sharply. On the other hand, if you hit the downstream end of the depression you will teeter on top of the wave or fall off the back side.

Next time you prepare for a ferry, think about your homework. Are you parallel to the eddy line? Close to the eddy line? What is the current direction immediately on the other side of the eddy line? How does it change as you go toward the middle of the river? Where on the eddy line do you want your bow to cross in order to hit the depression and slide out onto a surf wave? Taking the time to factor in these variables will guarantee you fewer failed ferries.

Dial in the angle, crank on forward speed, and target your attack on the surfing wave!

Reading Water: Scan the Road Ahead

Kent Ford

I remember my first day behind the wheel in driver's ed. Heading out the driveway of school, I had my eyes riveted on the hood of the car.

As the car ran up on the curb, the instructor grabbed the wheel, screaming for me to look down the road. I got a lengthy lecture on scanning the road.

Learning to paddle whitewater can be a similar experience. Reading the road and reading the river actually have a lot in common.

The key to reading water is to lift your vision! Don't just look at your bow. Look where you want to go and at what lies in between. What should you be looking for? Simply: easily visible rocks, water features created by rocks under the surface, and hazards.

You can spot rocks above the surface pretty easily and maneuver to get around them. If you don't quite make the move and you find yourself floating sideways toward one, the proper reaction is to lean your body and boat aggressively toward the rock, even putting your hand or paddle on it. The water buffeting off the rock forms a pillow which helps keep your boat off the rock. Learn to distinguish between round, friendly rocks and the more hazardous ones with a sharp upstream edge.

As you scan the rapid, look far downstream to determine the line of the current and where it ends. Does the main flow travel down one shore, then traverse to finish in a wave train on the other side? You see rocks above the water deflecting the current. Figure out why the current was deflected; that's the key to reading the rapid.

Rocks just under the surface have the same effect. Most of the water flow moves to avoid the barely submerged rock, leaving some water to pour over the rock. The resulting water feature is either a hole or a wave, depending on how much water is pouring over. Little water flowing over creates a strong eddy below and a very flat hole, often called a hydraulic. More water generates a hole, a wave-like formation with a white frothy backwash. Study rapids from different points on shore to determine what each feature looks like from varied points of view.

Occasionally, you will not be able to see the water as it disappears over the edge of a drop. This "horizon line" indicates a bigger drop, one that you will probably want to scout from shore. Look for the biggest waves in the main flow of current. Generally, those will guide you to a "clean" channel—and the most fun.

An instructor can help you learn to identify river hazards, like undercut rocks, or man-made obstructions like bridge pilings. Tree branches forming strainers, and against which a boat can be pinned by the full force of the river, are one of the most dangerous hazards in the sport. Scan for bouncing twigs and unexplained currents that might indicate a strainer. Learn to identify potential danger spots; then, concentrate your vision where you want to go, rather than fixating on what it is you want to avoid.

Learning to read water takes time and practice, so paddle within your ability and experience, and don't just follow the boat in front of you. Instead, explore safer rapids by picking your own line.

The Capistrano Flip

John Shepard

If you're paddling the way you should be—with exuberance and passion and a certain degree of abandon—before long you're going to capsize. When you do, here are two maneuvers for flat water that will set things right.

You suddenly find yourself in deep water beside your capsized canoe. The first order of business is to make sure your partner is all right and then to put on your PFD (which henceforth you'll have the wisdom to put on before you flip). If yours is the common vest type (Coast Guard Type III), float it upside down and opened up with the shoulders in front of you. Insert both arms in the arm holes, flip the

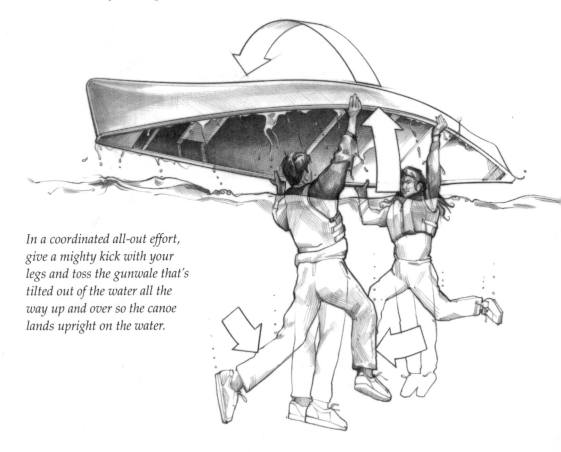

In a coordinated all-out effort, give a mighty kick with your legs and toss the gunwale that's tilted out of the water all the way up and over so the canoe lands upright on the water.

PFD over your head, and roll onto your back to zip and tie it.

Looking around, you notice that no other canoe is on hand to assist you. No matter. In your best Italian accent, suggest to your partner that the two of you orchestrate a Capistrano Flip.

Turn the canoe upside down and tread water with your head inside the air pocket underneath and your hands on the gunwales. Face your partner from opposite ends of the canoe. If solo, which makes things more difficult, position yourself in the middle of the boat.

To get as much of the canoe out of the water as possible, lift one gunwale and grab a "bite" of air while thrusting the other gunwale upward. Let the canoe rest on the surface of the water while you and your partner take a deep breath. Then, in an all-out effort coordinated precisely with your partner, break the air seal by lifting one gunwale just above the water surface, give a mighty kick with your legs, and toss the gunwale that's tilted out of the water all the way up and over so the canoe lands upright. Preventing the other gunwale

from dripping below the surface and scooping up water is critical to the success of this move. Under the best of circumstances, you still may need to do some bailing once you're back on board.

Having another canoe on hand makes matters easier, because you can do a canoe-over-canoe rescue. Position the swamped craft upside down and perpendicular to the center of the upright, "rescue" canoe. The bow rescuer turns around to face his or her partner (the canoe-over-canoe can also be performed by a solo rescuer), and one "victim" remains beside the swamped canoe. As the victim breaks the air seal of the swamped canoe, the rescuers lift the end closest to them and pass the canoe hand-over-hand across the gunwales of their boat. To compensate for the rescue canoe's tendency to tip toward the swamped canoe as it's lifted from the water, the second victim can steady the rescue canoe by holding onto the opposite gunwale.

Once emptied, the swamped canoe can be flipped upright and slid neatly back into the water, and you can carry on as exuberantly as before.

The Scoop on Rescues: Easier Re-entries

Laurie Gullion

Beginners tell me that their goal in canoeing is to avoid tipping over and to stay dry. But I can't guarantee them that they'll stay upright; getting wet is often a part of the sport. The fact is that most tipovers occur in shallow water, near shore, getting into and out of the canoe. Deep water capsizes are the exception.

That said, new paddlers need to develop rescue skills to keep pace with their paddling skills, and rescue practice is important from the beginning. Do your practice, first, in shallow water before moving on to deep water.

Rescue practice is a part of every hot-weather program I conduct for kids; they love to tip over and climb in and out of canoes, and I encourage them to go for a "personal best" in improving their rescue times. Every child gets to be both a rescuer and a "victim."

Knowing how to rescue a tipped canoe makes you a more confident paddler, and you can assist other people without getting into trouble yourself.

The reliable standard is called the "T" rescue (that's how the capsized canoe gets emptied), and I've watched a few paddlers master it quickly.

Many are able to execute it in less than two minutes. If the rescue stalls, it's pre-dictably at the point when swimmers (victims) try to re-enter their canoe. Clambering in over the gunwale in a cold-water scenario is extremely difficult for some paddlers.

In this scenario, rescuers have smoothly emptied the swamped boat of water and created a catamaran between the rescue canoe and the empty canoe. Now, their challenge is getting the swimmers back into the boat.

Athletic canoeists can use a scissors kick to vault themselves out of the water, drape their waists over the gunwale while they rest on straightened arms, and tuck one shoulder to roll into the boat or simply step over the gunwale. But less agile victims have difficulty propelling themselves high enough in the water and above the gunwale, losing the necessary leverage to get into the canoe.

Here are some quick tips for getting the victim into the canoe easily.

THE SCOOP

Let the gunwale drop closer to the water as the victim pushes down on it, allowing him/her to get his/her hips near the gunwale. As the victim begins to roll into the canoe over a tucked shoulder, push down on the gunwale nearest to you to right the canoe and "scoop" the victim into it.

If you drop the gunwale very low for a struggling swimmer, you'll scoop water as well as the victim. That's fine in reasonable amounts; just bail it out once the person is settled in the canoe.

One caution: be quick in righting the canoe, or the swimmers may roll it over, or you may scoop too much water so the canoe is essentially swamped. Then, you'll have to re-start the T rescue, and your swimmers get to spend a longer time in the water.

THE LOG ROLL

A variation on the scoop is a log roll. Rather than coming over the gunwale in a vertical position, have your victim position himself/herself along the side of the canoe where a thwart will not inhibit entry. Tilt the canoe sharply so that your victim can drape one arm and one leg over the gunwale. Help your victim by pulling him/her over the gunwale, so that he/she rolls, like a log, into the bottom of the boat.

The log roll is a wet rescue, meaning that water gets scooped with the swimmer, so bailing is necessary. Positioning in front of or behind the center thwart is important, so the paddler's head doesn't smack the gunwale upon entry.

During training for wilderness canoeing trips, we have practiced the log roll for rescuing unconscious victims. The victim simulates unconsciousness by remaining limp in the water as rescuers perform the log roll. The victims report twinges of discomfort as their hips roll over the gunwale, but all agree it's a slick rescue for an extreme situation. Message to rescuers: roll them quickly.

Let the gunwale drop closer to the water as the victim pushes down on it. Then, scoop!

Painless Portaging

John Shepard

Painless portaging. Can't be done? It can, if you know how to waddle and tilt, and how and where to bridge.

Say what?

Let's start with a scenario. In fact, let's consider the idea of a painless portage from the worst possible perspective: from beneath an 18-foot wood-and-canvas canoe that's been sopping up water all day through a crack in the keel. Never mind how that monstrosity got up there on your shoulders in the first place. For now, the pressing question is, "How do I carry this thing another 100 rods without my arms going to sleep forever and my shoulder blades collapsing into my rib cage?"

First, loosen up your pelvis and waddle. Belly dancers seem to have an edge over the rest of us when it comes to this, but we can learn. The trick is to exaggerate

When you grasp the gunwales, extend one hand in front of you and place the other on the opposite gunwale near your shoulder. Keeping your knees bent, with each step momentarily lift the canoe off your shoulders.

your hip movements when you walk so that the canoe lightly bounces on your shoulders. With each bounce the shoulders slightly decompress, allowing a little blood to flow, and you're momentarily reminded that your arms are still there.

You can augment the relief provided by waddling through tilting the canoe. While one hand remains extended along the gunwale in front of you to keep that behemoth balanced, the other slides back along its gunwale to your shoulder and momentarily lifts the canoe. You can almost hear those nerve synapses cheer as they merrily fire off their rounds in their newfound freedom.

Admittedly, during a long portage even the best waddlers need a break every now and then, and when they do, they bridge. One way to bridge is to call out to the pack-bearing companion who has agreed to accompany you on this long portage (an important ally) and request her assistance. You stop waddling and your partner stands facing you about 3 feet away. She reaches up to grasp the gunwales and guides the stern down to the ground. Then she locks her elbows to better support the weight of the canoe and, when she's communicated to you that she's ready, you step out from beneath your burden. You can rest for a moment, then re-shoulder the yoke, or you can assume the bridge position behind her so that she can take over the job.

A second way to bridge involves some help from Mother Nature. As you're waddling beneath your wood-and-canvas, you may glimpse an occasional hardwood tree with a fork about 10 feet off the ground that's stout enough and shaped so that it could support the overturned bow of your canoe. All you do is tilt the bow up, ease it into the crotch of the tree, and take a well-earned breather. The only thing you need be mindful of is damaging your canoe if the tree should sway in the wind.

Feel better? Now, get back under that canoe and keep on waddlin'.

Games Paddlers Play

Laurie Gullion

Teaching technical canoeing skills through play is an exciting, fast-paced experience, and the children will respond with enthusiasm. Kids are poised for action—lots of it—and their desires can be met by a parent or group leader tuned in to the effectiveness of play. Short, light-hearted exercises and activities meet a child's need for action, involvement, speed, challenge, and fun.

Safety can also be promoted through play. Organization and the establishment of clear areas for safe play are necessities. Keep the rules simple, because complex activities can get confusing, and safety may be jeopardized.

Many great game ideas come from a leader's experience in other leisure programs. The following activity is adapted from a childhood game that worked well for me in teaching Nordic skiing and also succeeded on a water playground.

SHIPWRECK

Establish a rectangular playing field with four sides delineated by buoys. Identify the four sides as "bow," "stern," "port," and "starboard." Beyond each side of the rectangle must be unobstructed water so that paddlers have a zone in which to slow down and stop without hitting obstacles or each other.

All paddlers begin the game within the contour of the rectangle. One person begins the game by calling out a direction, such as "port." All paddlers paddle to that side of the rectangle as fast as they can. The last person to cross the line gets to make the next call. In this way, the slower paddlers are not eliminated from the game. Don't get into the muddle of having "line judges"; just let those who need the practice continue to play.

Shipwreck can be spiced up with other call-outs that must be executed in the center of the rectangle. Players must be aware of other paddlers and maintain enough spacing so they don't collide with other boats. The last person or team to finish the command task has to make the next call. The call-outs require these actions:

BUDDY UP!

Two boats must get themselves side-by-side, facing in opposite directions. Two paddlers will have to pivot first and then move sideways until their boats touch. Kayakers need to be careful that they don't clobber their partner with the paddle.

PERSON OVERBOARD!

Paddlers must eject from their boats and complete a re-entry. Canoeists have to leap overboard without overturning their boats and re-enter without flipping. Kayakers usually end up with water in their boats and end up wallowing around for the rest of the game.

SHARK ATTACK!

Boats need to group up in teams of three or four, side-by-side for "safety." The leftover boat makes the next call.

OCTOPUS!

Canoeists slide onto their backs on the bottom of the boat and wave their arms and legs in the air (like waving tentacles; get it?). This teaches the low-center-of-gravity principle. Kayakers must roll over and up.

Make sure your playing field is large enough to allow the boats room to move, particularly when technical paddling skills are high. Be willing to stop the action to control excitement levels, and make sure paddlers are aware at all times of any boats that may need help.

Set up an aquatic playing field.

Canoe & Kayak Subscription Information

For more than 24 years, *Canoe & Kayak* magazine has been the world's leading paddlesports publication and resource for canoeing, kayaking and the full range of paddlesports. Full-color features capture both the beauty and tranquillity of the sport as well as the adventure and excitement—from family weekend trips to world expeditions, from calm water touring to whitewater adventures.

Published six times a year, *Canoe & Kayak* includes regular sections on technique, equipment reviews, services, destinations, health and fitness, and the environment, along with features about the people, ideas, issues, and events that shape the growing sport of paddling. Subscription includes the annual Buyer's Guide in the December issue.

To subscribe, call 1-800-678-5432, and ask for the "Subscription Special," (six issues for $15) or write: *Canoe & Kayak* magazine, P.O. Box 7011, Red Oak, IA 51591-4011.